Can Hank Sing?

by Dale Cooper
illustrated by CD Hullinger

PEARSON

Scott
Foresman

Editorial Offices: Glenview, Illinois • Parsippany, New Jersey • New York, New York
Sales Offices: Needham, Massachusetts • Duluth, Georgia • Glenview, Illinois
Coppell, Texas • Sacramento, California • Mesa, Arizona

Every effort has been made to secure permission and provide appropriate credit for photographic material. The publisher deeply regrets any omission and pledges to correct errors called to its attention in subsequent editions.

Unless otherwise acknowledged, all photographs are the property of Scott Foresman, a division of Pearson Education.

Photo locators denoted as follows: Top (T), Center (C), Bottom (B), Left (L), Right (R), Background (Bkgd)

Illustrations by CD Hullinger

Photograph 8 ©DK Images

ISBN: 0-328-13181-4

7 8 9 10 V010 14 13 12 11 10 09 08

"You sing every song so well!"
said Hank.

"Any bluebird can sing," said Jan.

"Maybe you were not singing enough," said Jan.

"But I sing more than ever!" said Hank.

"My song is so little,"
said Hank.
"I think it is a good song,"
said Jan.

5

"Are you sure it is a bluebird song?" said Hank.

"Well, is it your own song?" said Jan.

"Can a bluebird sing like
a rooster?" said Hank.
"As long as you sing
your own song!" said Jan.

Hank didn't have a voice just like any other bluebird. Think about your voice. A person's voice changes over time. Once you sounded like a baby. Now you sound like a child. And someday you will sound like an adult. Think of how many different ways you will sound in your life!